1000 BUILDING BLOCKS

ENGLISH VOCABULARY FOR LEVELS A1 TO B1

🔊))) Audio and ▶ Video Included

TESOLCREATIONS

1000 Building Blocks
English Vocabulary for Levels A1 to B1

Copyright Altiora Literary © 2025
Published June 23, 2025

Printed in the United States of America
ISBN 979-8-218-72240-1

Video Disclaimer:
The videos linked through QR codes in this book contain images and design elements licensed from Canva. These videos are for educational purposes only and are not for individual sale. All Canva content is used in accordance with Canva's Content License Agreement.

TESOLCREATIONS

Greetings,

Welcome to *1000 Building Blocks English Vocabulary for Levels A1 to B1*! This book helps ESL learners build a strong English foundation.

It focuses on **CEFR levels A1 (Beginner), A2 (High Beginner), and B1 (Low Intermediate)**. It offers a list of important everyday words. Each section has audio and video you can get by scanning QR codes. You can hear how to pronounce the words and see them used in real situations.

You can use this book for self-study, in class, or online. Just 30 minutes to one hour of practice a day will help you improve your English. We hope this book helps you speak English with confidence.

Special thanks to Hannah C. for proofreading and to Timothy A. for designing the book.

To Dad Keith — we remember you every day, especially on June 23rd.

Note: *Some words are on the list but not in the videos. These words are italicized.*

TESOLCREATIONS

TABLE OF CONTENTS

English A1 – B1 Vocabulary

1. I am... Self-introduction

Hello!

It is nice to meet you!

I am _____.

I am from _____.

I am _____ years old.

I am a _____.

I am _____.

How about you?

1. I am… Self-introduction

Hello!

It is nice to meet you!

I am _____.

I am from _____.

I am _____ years old.

I am a _____.

I am _____.

How about you?

2. The English Alphabet

Aa Bb Cc
Dd Ee Ff
Gg Hh Ii
Jj Kk Ll
Mm Nn Oo
Pp Qq Rr
Ss Tt Uu
Vv Ww Xx
Yy Zz

2. The English Alphabet

Aa Bb Cc
Dd Ee Ff
Gg Hh Ii
Jj Kk Ll
Mm Nn Oo
Pp Qq Rr
Ss Tt Uu
Vv Ww Xx
Yy Zz

3. Personal Information

name
first name
middle name
last name
full name / *complete name*
age
birthday
address
apartment (apt.)
street (st.)
city
state
country
zip code
phone number
language
gender
eye color
height
weight
email address
signature (sign)
identification card (ID)
passport
family members
hair color
job / work / occupation
marital status
nationality
race
religion

3. Personal Information

name
first name
middle name
last name
full name / complete name
age
birthday
address
apartment (apt.)
street (st.)
city
state
country
zip code
phone number
language
gender
eye color
height
weight
email address
signature (sign)
identification card (ID)
passport
family members
hair color
job / work / occupation
marital status
nationality
race
religion

4. Greetings

Good morning.

Good afternoon.

Good evening.

Good night.

Goodbye.

Hello!

Hi!

How are you?

It is nice to meet you!

It is nice to meet you too.

See you.

See you later.

See you soon.

Take care.

Have a good day!

4. Greetings

Good morning.

Good afternoon.

Good evening.

Good night.

Goodbye.

Hello!

Hi!

How are you?

It is nice to meet you!

It is nice to meet you too.

See you.

See you later.

See you soon.

Take care.

Have a good day!

5. Polite Expressions

Excuse me.

Please.

Sorry.

Thank you.

You're welcome.

5. Polite Expressions

Excuse me.

Please.

Sorry.

Thank you.

You're welcome.

6. Feelings

I am happy.
I feel happy.

angry / mad
bored
calm
confused
excited
happy
hungry
nervous
sad
scared
shy
sick
sleepy
thirsty
tired
worried

6. Feelings

I am happy.
I feel happy.

angry / mad
bored
calm
confused
excited
happy
hungry
nervous
sad
scared
shy
sick
sleepy
thirsty
tired
worried

7. Days

Sun - Sunday
Mon - Monday
Tue - Tuesday
Wed - Wednesday
Thu - Thursday
Fri - Friday
Sat - Saturday

7. Days

Sun - Sunday
Mon - Monday
Tue - Tuesday
Wed Wednesday
Thu - Thursday
Fri - Friday
Sat - Saturday

8. Months

Jan - January	Jan - January
Feb - February	Feb - February
Mar - March	Mar - March
Apr - April	Apr - April
May - May	May - May
Jun - June	Jun - June
Jul - July	Jul - July
Aug - August	Aug - August
Sep - September	Sep - September
Oct - October	Oct - October
Nov - November	Nov - November
Dec - December	Dec - December

9. Weather

cloudy	cloudy
foggy	foggy
rainy	rainy
snowy	snowy
stormy	stormy
sunny	sunny
windy	windy
cold	cold
cool	cool
hot	hot
humid	humid
lightning	lightning
thunder	thunder
warm	warm

10. Seasons

autumn or fall
spring
summer
winter

10. Seasons

autumn or fall
spring
summer
winter

11. Temperature

cool
cold
freezing
hot
warm

11. Temperature

cool
cold
freezing
hot
warm

12. Cardinal Numbers

1 - one
2 - two
3 - three
4 - four
5 - five
6 - six
7 - seven
8 - eight
9 - nine
10 - ten

12. Cardinal Numbers

1 - one
2 - two
3 - three
4 - four
5 - five
6 - six
7 - seven
8 - eight
9 - nine
10 - ten

12. Cardinal Numbers

12. Cardinal Numbers

11 - eleven	11 - eleven
12 - twelve	12 - twelve
13 - thirteen	13 - thirteen
14 - fourteen	14 - fourteen
15 - fifteen	15 - fifteen
16 - sixteen	16 - sixteen
17 - seventeen	17 - seventeen
18 - eighteen	18 - eighteen
19 - nineteen	19 - nineteen
20 - twenty	20 - twenty
21 - twenty-one	21 - twenty-one
22 - twenty-two	22 - twenty-two
23 - twenty-three	23 - twenty-three
24 - twenty-four	24 - twenty-four
25 - twenty-five	25 - twenty-five
26 - twenty-six	26 - twenty-six
27 - twenty-seven	27 - twenty-seven
28 - twenty-eight	28 - twenty-eight
29 - twenty-nine	29 - twenty-nine
30 - thirty	30 - thirty
31 - thirty-one	31 - thirty-one
32 - thirty-two	32 - thirty-two
33 - thirty-three	33 - thirty-three
34 - thirty-four	34 - thirty-four
35 - thirty-five	35 - thirty-five
36 - thirty-six	36 - thirty-six
37 - thirty-seven	37 - thirty-seven
38 - thirty-eight	38 - thirty-eight
39 - thirty-nine	39 - thirty-nine
40 - forty	40 - forty

12. Cardinal Numbers

41 - forty-one
42 - forty-two
43 - forty-three
44 - forty-four
45 - forty-five
46 - forty-six
47 - forty-seven
48 - forty-eight
49 - forty-nine
50 - fifty
51 - fifty-one
52 - fifty-two
53 - fifty-three
54 - fifty-four
55 - fifty-five
56 - fifty-six
57 - fifty-seven
58 - fifty-eight
59 - fifty-nine
60 - sixty
61 - sixty-one
62 - sixty-two
63 - sixty-three
64 - sixty-four
65 - sixty-five
66 - sixty-six
67 - sixty-seven
68 - sixty-eight
69 - sixty-nine
70 - seventy

12. Cardinal Numbers

41 - forty-one
42 - forty-two
43 - forty-three
44 - forty-four
45 - forty-five
46 - forty-six
47 - forty-seven
48 - forty-eight
49 - forty-nine
50 - fifty
51 - fifty-one
52 - fifty-two
53 - fifty-three
54 - fifty-four
55 - fifty-five
56 - fifty-six
57 - fifty-seven
58 - fifty-eight
59 - fifty-nine
60 - sixty
61 - sixty-one
62 - sixty-two
63 - sixty-three
64 - sixty-four
65 - sixty-five
66 - sixty-six
67 - sixty-seven
68 - sixty-eight
69 - sixty-nine
70 - seventy

12. Cardinal Numbers

71 - seventy-one
72 - seventy-two
73 - seventy-three
74 - seventy-four
75 - seventy-five
76 - seventy-six
77 - seventy-seven
78 - seventy-eight
79 - seventy-nine
80 - eighty
81 - eighty-one
82 - eighty-two
83 - eighty-three
84 - eighty-four
85 - eighty-five
86 - eighty-six
87 - eighty-seven
88 - eighty-eight
89 - eighty-nine
90 - ninety
91 - ninety-one
92 - ninety-two
93 - ninety-three
94 - ninety-four
95 - ninety-five
96 - ninety-six
97 - ninety-seven
98 - ninety-eight
99 - ninety-nine
100 - one hundred

12. Cardinal Numbers

71 - seventy-one
72 - seventy-two
73 - seventy-three
74 - seventy-four
75 - seventy-five
76 - seventy-six
77 - seventy-seven
78 - seventy-eight
79 - seventy-nine
80 - eighty
81 - eighty-one
82 - eighty-two
83 - eighty-three
84 - eighty-four
85 - eighty-five
86 - eighty-six
87 - eighty-seven
88 - eighty-eight
89 - eighty-nine
90 - ninety
91 - ninety-one
92 - ninety-two
93 - ninety-three
94 - ninety-four
95 - ninety-five
96 - ninety-six
97 - ninety-seven
98 - ninety-eight
99 - ninety-nine
100 - one hundred

12. Cardinal Numbers

1,000 - one thousand
10,000 - ten thousand
100,000 - one hundred thousand
1,000,000 - one million

12. Cardinal Numbers

1,000 - one thousand
10,000 - ten thousand
100,000 - one hundred thousand
1,000,000 - one million

13. Ordinal Numbers

1st – first
2nd – second
3rd – third
4th – fourth
5th – fifth
6th – sixth
7th – seventh
8th – eighth
9th – ninth
10th – tenth
11th - eleventh
12th - twelfth
13th - thirteenth
14th - fourteenth
15th - fifteenth
16th - sixteenth
17th - seventeenth
18th - eighteenth
19th - nineteenth
20th - twentieth

13. Ordinal Numbers

1st – first
2nd – second
3rd – third
4th – fourth
5th – fifth
6th – sixth
7th – seventh
8th – eighth
9th – ninth
10th – tenth
11th - eleventh
12th - twelfth
13th - thirteenth
14th - fourteenth
15th - fifteenth
16th - sixteenth
17th - seventeenth
18th - eighteenth
19th - nineteenth
20th - twentieth

13. Ordinal Numbers

21st - twenty-first
22nd - twenty-second
23rd - twenty-third
24th - twenty-fourth
25th - twenty-fifth
26th - twenty-sixth
27th - twenty-seventh
28th - twenty-eighth
29th - twenty-ninth
30th - thirtieth
31st - thirty-first
32nd - thirty-second
33rd - thirty-third
34th - thirty-fourth
35th - thirty-fifth
36th - thirty-sixth
37th - thirty-seventh
38th - thirty-eighth
39th - thirty-ninth
40th - fortieth
41st - forty-first
42nd - forty-second
43rd - forty-third
44th - forty-fourth
45th - forty-fifth

13. Ordinal Numbers

21st - twenty-first
22nd - twenty-second
23rd - twenty-third
24th - twenty-fourth
25th - twenty-fifth
26th - twenty-sixth
27th - twenty-seventh
28th - twenty-eighth
29th - twenty-ninth
30th - thirtieth
31st - thirty-first
32nd - thirty-second
33rd - thirty-third
34th - thirty-fourth
35th - thirty-fifth
36th - thirty-sixth
37th - thirty-seventh
38th - thirty-eighth
39th - thirty-ninth
40th - fortieth
41st - forty-first
42nd - forty-second
43rd - forty-third
44th - forty-fourth
45th - forty-fifth

13. Ordinal Numbers

46th - forty-sixth

47th - forty-seventh

48th - forty-eighth

49th - forty-ninth

50th - fiftieth

51st - fifty-first

52nd - fifty-second

53rd - fifty-third

54th - fifty-fourth

55th - fifty-fifth

56th - fifty-sixth

57th - fifty-seventh

58th - fifty-eighth

59th - fifty-ninth

60th - sixtieth

61st - sixty-first

62nd - sixty-second

63rd - sixty-third

64th - sixty-fourth

65th - sixty-fifth

66th - sixty-sixth

67th - sixty-seventh

68th - sixty-eighth

69th - sixty-ninth

70th - seventieth

13. Ordinal Numbers

46th - forty-sixth

47th - forty-seventh

48th - forty-eighth

49th - forty-ninth

50th - fiftieth

51st - fifty-first

52nd - fifty-second

53rd - fifty-third

54th - fifty-fourth

55th - fifty-fifth

56th - fifty-sixth

57th - fifty-seventh

58th - fifty-eighth

59th - fifty-ninth

60th - sixtieth

61st - sixty-first

62nd - sixty-second

63rd - sixty-third

64th - sixty-fourth

65th - sixty-fifth

66th - sixty-sixth

67th - sixty-seventh

68th - sixty-eighth

69th - sixty-ninth

70th - seventieth

13. Ordinal Numbers

71st - seventy-first

72nd - seventy-second

73rd - seventy-third

74th - seventy-fourth

75th - seventy-fifth

76th - seventy-sixth

77th - seventy-seventh

78th - seventy-eighth

79th - seventy-ninth

80th - eightieth

81st – eighty-first

82nd – eighty-second

83rd – eighty-third

84th – eighty-fourth

85th – eighty-fifth

86th – eighty-sixth

87th - eighty-seventh

88th - eighty-eighth

89th - eighty-ninth

90th - ninetieth

91st - ninety-first

92nd - ninety-second

93rd - ninety-third

94th - ninety-fourth

95th - ninety-fifth

96th - ninety-sixth

13. Ordinal Numbers

71st - seventy-first

72nd - seventy-second

73rd - seventy-third

74th - seventy-fourth

75th - seventy-fifth

76th - seventy-sixth

77th - seventy-seventh

78th - seventy-eighth

79th - seventy-ninth

80th - eightieth

81st – eighty-first

82nd – eighty-second

83rd – eighty-third

84th – eighty-fourth

85th – eighty-fifth

86th – eighty-sixth

87th - eighty-seventh

88th - eighty-eighth

89th - eighty-ninth

90th - ninetieth

91st - ninety-first

92nd - ninety-second

93rd - ninety-third

94th - ninety-fourth

95th - ninety-fifth

96th - ninety-sixth

13. Ordinal Numbers

97th - ninety-seventh
98th - ninety-eighth
99th - ninety-ninth
100th - one hundredth
1,000th - one thousandth
10,000th - ten thousandth
100,000th - one hundred thousandth
1,000,000th - one millionth

13. Ordinal Numbers

97th - ninety-seventh
98th - ninety-eighth
99th - ninety-ninth
100th - one hundredth
1,000th - one thousandth
10,000th - ten thousandth
100,000th - one hundred thousandth
1,000,000th - one millionth

14. Calendar

appointment
date
day
month
schedule
season
today
tomorrow
week
weekday
weekend
year
yesterday

14. Calendar

appointment
date
day
month
schedule
season
today
tomorrow
week
weekday
weekend
year
yesterday

15. Time

15. Time

AM	AM
PM	PM
alarm	alarm
clock	clock
hour	hour
minute	minute
second	second
timer	timer
watch	watch
sunrise	sunrise
sunset	sunset
morning	morning
noon	noon
afternoon	afternoon
evening	evening
night	night
midnight	midnight
dawn	dawn
dusk	dusk
12 a.m. - twelve a.m. / midnight	12 a.m. - twelve a.m. / midnight
1 a.m. - one a.m.	1 a.m. - one a.m.
2 a.m. - two a.m.	2 a.m. - two a.m.
3 a.m. - three a.m.	3 a.m. - three a.m.
4 a.m. - four a.m.	4 a.m. - four a.m.
5 a.m. - five a.m.	5 a.m. - five a.m.
6 a.m. - six a.m.	6 a.m. - six a.m.
7 a.m. - seven a.m.	7 a.m. - seven a.m.
8 a.m. - eight a.m.	8 a.m. - eight a.m.

15. Time

9 a.m. - nine a.m.

10 a.m. - ten a.m.

11 a.m. - eleven a.m.

12 p.m. - twelve p.m. / noon

1 p.m. - one p.m.

2 p.m. - two p.m.

3 p.m. - three p.m.

4 p.m. - four p.m.

5 p.m. - five p.m.

6 p.m. - six p.m.

7 p.m. - seven p.m.

8 p.m. - eight p.m.

9 p.m. - nine p.m.

10 p.m. - ten p.m.

11 p.m. - eleven p.m.

1:00 - one o'clock

1:01 - one oh one

1:02 - one oh two

1:03 - one oh three

1:04 - one oh four

1:05 - one oh five

1:06 - one oh six

1:07 - one oh seven

1:08 - one oh eight

1:09 - one oh nine

1:10 - one ten

15. Time

9 a.m. - nine a.m.

10 a.m. - ten a.m.

11 a.m. - eleven a.m.

12 p.m. - twelve p.m. / noon

1 p.m. - one p.m.

2 p.m. - two p.m.

3 p.m. - three p.m.

4 p.m. - four p.m.

5 p.m. - five p.m.

6 p.m. - six p.m.

7 p.m. - seven p.m.

8 p.m. - eight p.m.

9 p.m. - nine p.m.

10 p.m. - ten p.m.

11 p.m. - eleven p.m.

1:00 - one o'clock

1:01 - one oh one

1:02 - one oh two

1:03 - one oh three

1:04 - one oh four

1:05 - one oh five

1:06 - one oh six

1:07 - one oh seven

1:08 - one oh eight

1:09 - one oh nine

1:10 - one ten

15. Time

1:11 - one eleven

1:12 - one twelve

1:13 - one thirteen

1:14 - one fourteen

1:15 - one fifteen

1:16 - one sixteen

1:17 - one seventeen

1:18 - one eighteen

1:19 - one nineteen

1:20 - one twenty

1:21 - one twenty-one

1:22 - one twenty-two

1:23 - one twenty-three

1:24 - one twenty-four

1:25 - one twenty-five

1:26 - one twenty-six

1:27 - one twenty-seven

1:28 - one twenty-eight

1:29 - one twenty-nine

1:30 - one thirty

1:31 - one thirty-one

1:32 - one thirty-two

1:33 - one thirty-three

1:34 - one thirty-four

1:35 - one thirty-five

15. Time

1:11 - one eleven

1:12 - one twelve

1:13 - one thirteen

1:14 - one fourteen

1:15 - one fifteen

1:16 - one sixteen

1:17 - one seventeen

1:18 - one eighteen

1:19 - one nineteen

1:20 - one twenty

1:21 - one twenty-one

1:22 - one twenty-two

1:23 - one twenty-three

1:24 - one twenty-four

1:25 - one twenty-five

1:26 - one twenty-six

1:27 - one twenty-seven

1:28 - one twenty-eight

1:29 - one twenty-nine

1:30 - one thirty

1:31 - one thirty-one

1:32 - one thirty-two

1:33 - one thirty-three

1:34 - one thirty-four

1:35 - one thirty-five

15. Time

1:36 - one thirty-six

1:37 - one thirty-seven

1:38 - one thirty-eight

1:39 - one thirty-nine

1:40 - one forty

1:41 - one forty-one

1:42 - one forty-two

1:43 - one forty-three

1:44 - one forty-four

1:45 - one forty-five

1:46 - one forty-six

1:47 - one forty-seven

1:48 - one forty-eight

1:49 - one forty-nine

1:50 - one fifty

1:51 - one fifty-one

1:52 - one fifty-two

1:53 - one fifty-three

1:54 - one fifty-four

1:55 - one fifty-five

1:55 - one fifty-five

1:56 - one fifty-six

1:57 - one fifty-seven

1:58 - one fifty-eight

1:59 - one fifty-nine

2:00 pm - two p.m. / 2 o'clock

15. Time

1:36 - one thirty-six

1:37 - one thirty-seven

1:38 - one thirty-eight

1:39 - one thirty-nine

1:40 - one forty

1:41 - one forty-one

1:42 - one forty-two

1:43 - one forty-three

1:44 - one forty-four

1:45 - one forty-five

1:46 - one forty-six

1:47 - one forty-seven

1:48 - one forty-eight

1:49 - one forty-nine

1:50 - one fifty

1:51 - one fifty-one

1:52 - one fifty-two

1:53 - one fifty-three

1:54 - one fifty-four

1:55 - one fifty-five

1:55 - one fifty-five

1:56 - one fifty-six

1:57 - one fifty-seven

1:58 - one fifty-eight

1:59 - one fifty-nine

2:00 pm - two p.m. / 2 o'clock

16. Body Parts

16. Body Parts

ankle	ankle
arm	arm
back	back
cheek	cheek
chest	chest
chin	chin
ear	ear
elbow	elbow
eye	eye
eyebrow	eyebrow
face	face
finger	finger
foot / *feet*	foot / feet
forehead	forehead
hand	hand
hair	hair
head	head
heel	heel
hip	hip
knee	knee
leg	leg
lip	lip
mouth	mouth
neck	neck
nose	nose
palm	palm

16. Body Parts

shoulder

skin

stomach

thigh

toe

tongue

tooth / *teeth*

wrist

armpit

eyelash

jaw

16. Body Parts

shoulder

skin

stomach

thigh

toe

tongue

tooth / teeth

wrist

armpit

eyelash

jaw

17. Health Problems

allergy

backache

cough

cold

earache

fever

headache

nausea

rash

runny nose

sore throat

sprain

17. Health Problems

allergy

backache

cough

cold

earache

fever

headache

nausea

rash

runny nose

sore throat

sprain

17. Health Problems

stomachache

toothache

vomit

broken bone

bruise

burn

chest pain

cut

sunburn

17. Health Problems

stomachache

toothache

vomit

broken bone

bruise

burn

chest pain

cut

sunburn

18. Health Words

appointment

checkup

clinic

doctor

emergency

hospital

medicine

nurse

pain

patient

pill

sick

18. Health Words

appointment

checkup

clinic

doctor

emergency

hospital

medicine

nurse

pain

patient

pill

sick

19. Healthy Habits

breathe

brush

drink

eat

exercise

jog

jump

nap

play

rest

run

sleep

stretch

swim

walk

wash

19. Healthy Habits

breathe

brush

drink

eat

exercise

jog

jump

nap

play

rest

run

sleep

stretch

swim

walk

wash

20. Daily Routine For Non-Working Adults

brush my teeth

clean my house

comb my hair

cook breakfast

cook lunch

cook dinner

20. Daily Routine For Non-Working Adults

brush my teeth

clean my house

comb my hair

cook breakfast

cook lunch

cook dinner

20. Daily Routine For Non-Working Adults

do my assignments /
 do my homework
do the laundry
drive my child to school
drive to school
eat breakfast
eat lunch
eat dinner
exercise
feed my children
fold clothes
get dressed
go home
go to a doctor's
 appointment
go to the park
make my bed
pick up my children from
 school
play with my family
pray
rest
shop
sleep
study

20. Daily Routine For Non-Working Adults

do my assignments /
 do my homework
do the laundry
drive my child to school
drive to school
eat breakfast
eat lunch
eat dinner
exercise
feed my children
fold clothes
get dressed
go home
go to a doctor's
 appointment
go to the park
make my bed
pick up my children from
 school
play with my family
pray
rest
shop
sleep
study

20. Daily Routine For Non-Working Adults

take a bath / *shower*

take a nap

take care of my children

take my children to school

use the internet

vacuum the floor

visit my family

visit my friends

wake up

walk my dog

walk to school

watch TV

wash dishes

20. Daily Routine For Non-Working Adults

take a bath / shower

take a nap

take care of my children

take my children to school

use the internet

vacuum the floor

visit my family

visit my friends

wake up

walk my dog

walk to school

watch TV

wash dishes

21. Daily Routine For Working Adults

arrange

arrive

build

carry

check

clean

clock in

clock out

21. Daily Routine For Working Adults

arrange

arrive

build

carry

check

clean

clock in

clock out

21. Daily Routine
For Working Adults

deliver	deliver
drive	drive
fill up	fill up
finish my work	finish my work
fix	fix
go home	go home
go to work	go to work
help	help
load	load
make coffee	make coffee
pack lunch	pack lunch
pick	pick
receive	receive
scan	scan
shave	shave
shower	shower
start my work	start my work
take a lunch break	take a lunch break
take a bus	take a bus
take a train	take a train
use	use
wrap	wrap

21. Daily Routine
For Working Adults

22. Hobbies

baking	baking
cooking	cooking
crafting	crafting
cycling	cycling
dancing	dancing
drawing	drawing
driving	driving
fishing	fishing
gardening	gardening
hiking	hiking
jogging	jogging
knitting	knitting
listening to music	listening to music
painting	painting
playing sports	playing sports
reading	reading
sewing	sewing
singing	singing
swimming	swimming
traveling	traveling
watching movies	watching movies
writing	writing

23. Sports

archery	archery
badminton	badminton
baseball	baseball
basketball	basketball
bowling	bowling
boxing	boxing
cycling	cycling
fencing	fencing
football	football
golf	golf
gymnastics	gymnastics
hockey	hockey
rugby	rugby
running	running
skating	skating
skiing	skiing
soccer	soccer
swimming	swimming
table tennis	table tennis
tennis	tennis
volleyball	volleyball
wrestling	wrestling

23. Sports

24. Family Members

24. Family Members

aunt	aunt
baby	baby
brother	brother
cousin	cousin
daughter	daughter
father	father
parent	parent
grandchild	grandchild
granddaughter	granddaughter
grandson	grandson
grandchildren	grandchildren
grandfather	grandfather
grandparent	grandparent
grandmother	grandmother
grandparents	grandparents
husband	husband
spouse	spouse
mother	mother
parent	parent
parents	parents
nephew	nephew
niece	niece
sister	sister
sibling	sibling
siblings	siblings

24. Family Members

son

uncle

wife

older brother

younger brother

older sister

younger sister

twin

father-in-law

mother-in-law

step brother

step sister

24. Family Members

son

uncle

wife

older brother

younger brother

older sister

younger sister

twin

father-in-law

mother-in-law

step brother

step sister

25. House/ Home

attic

balcony

basement

bathroom

bedroom

ceiling

chimney

closet

dining room

25. House/ Home

attic

balcony

basement

bathroom

bedroom

ceiling

chimney

closet

dining room

25. House/ Home

doorknob	doorknob
entrance	entrance
fence	fence
fireplace	fireplace
floor	floor
garage	garage
garden	garden
hallway	hallway
home office	home office
kitchen	kitchen
laundry room	laundry room
living room	living room
pantry	pantry
roof	roof
stairs	stairs
wall	wall
window	window
yard	yard

26. Things at Home

Living Room

- air conditioner

Living Room

- air conditioner

26. Things at Home

Living Room

- bench
- carpet
- clock
- couch
- cushion
- curtain
- fan
- fireplace
- lamp
- mirror
- plant
- rug
- table
- television
- television remote
- vase
- window

Bedroom

- alarm clock
- bed
- blanket
- bookcase
- chair
- clothes

26. Things at Home

Living Room

- bench
- carpet
- clock
- couch
- cushion
- curtain
- fan
- fireplace
- lamp
- mirror
- plant
- rug
- table
- television
- television remote
- vase
- window

Bedroom

- alarm clock
- bed
- blanket
- bookcase
- chair
- clothes

26. Things at Home

Bedroom

- closet
- curtain
- drawer
- dresser
- hanger
- lamp
- picture frame
- pillow
- table
- toy
- wardrobe
- window

Dining Room

- bowl
- candle
- chair
- cup
- flower
- fork
- glass
- knife

26. Things at Home

Bedroom

- closet
- curtain
- drawer
- dresser
- hanger
- lamp
- picture frame
- pillow
- table
- toy
- wardrobe
- window

Dining Room

- bowl
- candle
- chair
- cup
- flower
- fork
- glass
- knife

26. Things at Home

- lamp
- picture frame
- plate
- pitcher
- saucer
- spoon
- table
- teaspoon

Kitchen

- bottle
- bowl
- cabinet
- can opener
- cup
- cutting board
- dish washer
- electric kettle
- kettle
- fork
- glass
- knife
- juicer
- measuring cup

26. Things at Home

- lamp
- picture frame
- plate
- pitcher
- saucer
- spoon
- table
- teaspoon

Kitchen

- bottle
- bowl
- cabinet
- can opener
- cup
- cutting board
- dish washer
- electric kettle
- kettle
- fork
- glass
- knife
- juicer
- measuring cup

26. Things at Home

- measuring spoon
- microwave oven
- mixer
- mug
- napkin
- oven
- pan
- peeler
- plate
- pot
- rice cooker
- rolling pin
- sink
- spice
- spoon
- stove
- strainer
- toaster
- tongs
- water dispenser
- whisk
- *refrigerator*

26. Things at Home

- measuring spoon
- microwave oven
- mixer
- mug
- napkin
- oven
- pan
- peeler
- plate
- pot
- rice cooker
- rolling pin
- sink
- spice
- spoon
- stove
- strainer
- toaster
- tongs
- water dispenser
- whisk
- refrigerator

26. Things at Home

Bathroom

- bathtub
- bucket
- conditioner
- faucet
- light
- laundry basket
- mat
- mirror
- plunger
- shampoo
- shower
- shower curtain
- sink
- soap
- toilet
- toilet paper
- tooth brush
- tooth paste
- towel
- washing machine
- window

26. Things at Home

Bathroom

- bathtub
- bucket
- conditioner
- faucet
- light
- laundry basket
- mat
- mirror
- plunger
- shampoo
- shower
- shower curtain
- sink
- soap
- toilet
- toilet paper
- tooth brush
- tooth paste
- towel
- washing machine
- window

26. Things at Home

Cleaning Supplies

- broom
- bucket
- brush
- detergent
- duster
- dustpan
- gloves
- laundry basket
- mop
- rag
- sponge
- trash can / *garbage can*

26. Things at Home

Cleaning Supplies

- broom
- bucket
- brush
- detergent
- duster
- dustpan
- gloves
- laundry basket
- mop
- rag
- sponge
- trash can / garbage can

27. Home Expenses

- education (school fees, supplies)
- entertainment (dining out, movies)
- groceries
- healthcare (insurance, medicine)
- housing (rent/mortgage)

27. Home Expenses

- education (school fees, supplies)
- entertainment (dining out, movies)
- groceries
- healthcare (insurance, medicine)
- housing (rent/mortgage)

27. Home Expenses

- miscellaneous (furniture, appliances, clothing, household items)
- savings
- transportation (gas, public transit)
- utilities (electricity, water, gas)

27. Home Expenses

- miscellaneous (furniture, appliances, clothing, household items)
- savings
- transportation (gas, public transit)
- utilities (electricity, water, gas)

28. Classroom English

assignment / homework

answer

choose

circle the letter

classmate

close your book

difficult/hard

easy

finish

help

listen

look

make groups

28. Classroom English

assignment / homework

answer

choose

circle the letter

classmate

close your book

difficult/hard

easy

finish

help

listen

look

make groups

28. Classroom English

open your book

pair up

question

raise your hand

read

ready

repeat

say

sit

stand

start

student

talk

teacher

test

turn to page

write

partner

work together

28. Classroom English

open your book

pair up

question

raise your hand

read

ready

repeat

say

sit

stand

start

student

talk

teacher

test

turn to page

write

partner

work together

29. School Supplies

backpack

bag

binder

29. School Supplies

backpack

bag

binder

29. School Supplies

binder clip	binder clip
book	book
chair	chair
chalk	chalk
clock	clock
computer	computer
crayon	crayon
desk	desk
envelope	envelope
eraser	eraser
folder	folder
globe	globe
glue	glue
highlighter	highlighter
laptop	laptop
marker	marker
notebook	notebook
paper	paper
paper clip	paper clip
pen	pen
pencil	pencil
pencil case	pencil case
pencil sharpener	pencil sharpener
projector	projector
puncher	puncher
hole puncher	hole puncher

29. School Supplies

ruler	ruler
scissors	scissors
stapler	stapler
table	table
tape	tape
trash can	trash can
whiteboard	whiteboard
box	box
calculator	calculator
key	key
magazine	magazine
newspaper	newspaper

30. Computer Words

app (application)	app (application)
Bluetooth	Bluetooth
browser	browser
cable	cable
Central Processing Unit (CPU)	Central Processing Unit (CPU)
compact disc (CD)	compact disc (CD)
computer	computer
charger	charger

30. Computer Words

download	download
email	email
external hard drive	external hard drive
file	file
flash drive	flash drive
folder	folder
icon	icon
internet	internet
keyboard	keyboard
laptop	laptop
memory card (SD card)	memory card (SD card)
microphone	microphone
modem	modem
mouse	mouse
printer	printer
router	router
scanner	scanner
software	software
speaker	speaker
update	update
upload	upload
webcam	webcam
website	website
Wi-Fi	Wi-Fi

31. Places at School

auditorium	auditorium
cafeteria	cafeteria
classroom	classroom
clinic	clinic
computer lab	computer lab
entrance	entrance
gym	gym
hallway	hallway
library	library
locker room	locker room
office	office
playground	playground
restroom	restroom
science lab	science lab

32. Jobs/Work

baker	baker
barber	barber
bus driver	bus driver
business owner	business owner
carpenter	carpenter
cashier	cashier
chef	chef

32. Jobs/Work

32. Jobs/Work

cleaner	cleaner
construction worker	construction worker
courier	courier
custodian	custodian
delivery driver	delivery driver
dentist	dentist
doctor	doctor
electrician	electrician
employee	employee
employer	employer
engineer	engineer
factory worker	factory worker
farmer	farmer
firefighter	firefighter
flight attendant	flight attendant
gardener	gardener
hairdresser	hairdresser
hairstylist	hairstylist
janitor	janitor
judge	judge
lawyer	lawyer
librarian	librarian
mail carrier	mail carrier
manager	manager
mechanic	mechanic
nurse	nurse

32. Jobs/Work

pharmacist

photographer

pilot

plumber

police officer

receptionist

scientist

secretary

security guard

server

social worker

soldier

staff

tailor

taxi driver

teacher

truck driver

veterinarian (vet)

32. Jobs/Work

pharmacist

photographer

pilot

plumber

police officer

receptionist

scientist

secretary

security guard

server

social worker

soldier

staff

tailor

taxi driver

teacher

truck driver

veterinarian (vet)

33. Places

Man-Made Places

- alley
- airport

33. Places

Man-Made Places

- alley
- airport

33. Places

Man-Made Places

- apartment
- avenue
- bank
- barbershop
- block
- bookstore
- building
- bridge
- bus station
- cafeteria
- café
- castle
- church
- city
- clinic
- convenience store
- country
- fire station
- flower shop
- gas station
- grocery store
- gym
- hospital
- hotel
- house

33. Places

Man-Made Places

- apartment
- avenue
- bank
- barbershop
- block
- bookstore
- building
- bridge
- bus station
- cafeteria
- café
- castle
- church
- city
- clinic
- convenience store
- country
- fire station
- flower shop
- gas station
- grocery store
- gym
- hospital
- hotel
- house

33. Places

Man-Made Places

- library
- mall
- monument
- mosque
- museum
- office
- park
- pet store
- pharmacy
- police station
- post office
- restroom
- restaurant
- school
- state
- street
- subway
- supermarket
- temple
- theater
- town
- train station
- village
- zoo

33. Places

Man-Made Places

- library
- mall
- monument
- mosque
- museum
- office
- park
- pet store
- pharmacy
- police station
- post office
- restroom
- restaurant
- school
- state
- street
- subway
- supermarket
- temple
- theater
- town
- train station
- village
- zoo

33. Places

Natural Places

- beach
- canyon
- desert
- forest
- hill
- island
- lake
- mountain
- ocean
- plateau
- river
- sea
- valley

33. Places

Natural Places

- beach
- canyon
- desert
- forest
- hill
- island
- lake
- mountain
- ocean
- plateau
- river
- sea
- valley

34. Transportation

Land transportation

- ambulance
- bicycle (bike)
- bus
- car
- motorcycle
- scooter
- taxi
- train

34. Transportation

Land transportation

- ambulance
- bicycle (bike)
- bus
- car
- motorcycle
- scooter
- taxi
- train

34. Transportation

- tricycle
- truck
- van

Air transportation

- airplane
- helicopter
- hot air balloon

Water transportation

- boat
- ferry
- ship

34. Transportation

- tricycle
- truck
- van

Air transportation

- airplane
- helicopter
- hot air balloon

Water transportation

- boat
- ferry
- ship

35. Money

Bills

- $1 - one dollar
- $5 - five dollars
- $10 - ten dollars
- $20 - twenty dollars
- $50 - fifty dollars
- $100 - one hundreds

Coins

- 1¢ - one cent or penny
- 5¢ - five cents or nickel

35. Money

Bills

- $1 - one dollar
- $5 - five dollars
- $10 - ten dollars
- $20 - twenty dollars
- $50 - fifty dollars
- $100 - one hundreds

Coins

- 1¢ - one cent or penny
- 5¢ - five cents or nickel

35. Money

Coins

- 10¢ - ten cents or dime
- 25¢ - twenty-five cents or quarter

35. Money

Coins

- 10¢ - ten cents or dime
- 25¢ - twenty-five cents or quarter

36. Banking Words

- ATM (Automated Teller Machine)
- bank
- bill
- cash
- coin
- credit card
- currency
- debit card
- deposit
- dollar
- fee
- loan
- money
- paycheck
- PIN (Personal Identification Number)
- receipt

36. Banking Words

- ATM (Automated Teller Machine)
- bank
- bill
- cash
- coin
- credit card
- currency
- debit card
- deposit
- dollar
- fee
- loan
- money
- paycheck
- PIN (Personal Identification Number)
- receipt

36. Banking Words

- rent
- salary
- save
- spend
- tax
- wage
- withdraw

36. Banking Words

- rent
- salary
- save
- spend
- tax
- wage
- withdraw

37. Credit and Debit Card Information

- bank name
- card brand
- card number
- card type
- cardholder name
- chip
- expiration date
- hologram
- security code
- signature box

37. Credit and Debit Card Information

- bank name
- card brand
- card number
- card type
- cardholder name
- chip
- expiration date
- hologram
- security code
- signature box

38. Colors

black

blue

brown

gold

gray

green

indigo

orange

pink

purple

red

silver

violet

white

yellow

38. Colors

black

blue

brown

gold

gray

green

indigo

orange

pink

purple

red

silver

violet

white

yellow

39. Shapes

circle

diamond

heart

oval

rectangle

square

star

triangle

39. Shapes

circle

diamond

heart

oval

rectangle

square

star

triangle

40. Shopping

Clothes

- blazer
- blouse
- coat
- dress
- hoodie
- jeans
- jacket
- pajama
- pants
- raincoat
- shirt
- shorts
- skirt
- socks
- suit
- sweater
- t-shirt
- uniform

Footwear

- boots
- flip-flops
- sandals
- shoes
- slippers

Clothes

- blazer
- blouse
- coat
- dress
- hoodie
- jeans
- jacket
- pajama
- pants
- raincoat
- shirt
- shorts
- skirt
- socks
- suit
- sweater
- t-shirt
- uniform

Footwear

- boots
- flip-flops
- sandals
- shoes
- slippers

40. Shopping

Accessories

- backpack
- belt
- button
- cap
- earrings
- eye glasses
- gloves
- hat
- necklace
- pocket
- purse
- scarf
- shawl
- sunglasses
- tie
- umbrella
- wallet
- watch

Self-Care

- body wash
- cologne
- comb
- conditioner
- cotton swabs
- dental floss

40. Shopping

Accessories

- backpack
- belt
- button
- cap
- earrings
- eye glasses
- gloves
- hat
- necklace
- pocket
- purse
- scarf
- shawl
- sunglasses
- tie
- umbrella
- wallet
- watch

Self-Care

- body wash
- cologne
- comb
- conditioner
- cotton swabs
- dental floss

40. Shopping

Self-Care

- deodorant
- hairbrush
- hairdryer
- hair gel
- hand sanitizer
- lotion
- mirror
- mouthwash
- nail clippers
- perfume
- razor
- shampoo
- shaving cream
- soap
- sunscreen
- tissue
- toilet paper
- toothbrush
- toothpaste
- tweezers
- wet wipes

40. Shopping

Self-Care

- deodorant
- hairbrush
- hairdryer
- hair gel
- hand sanitizer
- lotion
- mirror
- mouthwash
- nail clippers
- perfume
- razor
- shampoo
- shaving cream
- soap
- sunscreen
- tissue
- toilet paper
- toothbrush
- toothpaste
- tweezers
- wet wipes

41. Fruits

apple

avocado

41. Fruits

apple

avocado

41. Fruits

banana

blackberry

blueberry

cherry

coconut

date

fig

grape

guava

kiwi

lemon

lime

mango

melon

nectarine

olive

orange

papaya

passion fruit

peach

pear

persimmon

pineapple

plum

pomegranate

raisin

raspberry

41. Fruits

banana

blackberry

blueberry

cherry

coconut

date

fig

grape

guava

kiwi

lemon

lime

mango

melon

nectarine

olive

orange

papaya

passion fruit

peach

pear

persimmon

pineapple

plum

pomegranate

raisin

raspberry

41. Fruits

soursop

starfruit

strawberry

tangerine

tomato

watermelon

41. Fruits

soursop

starfruit

strawberry

tangerine

tomato

watermelon

42. Vegetables

asparagus

bean

beet

bell pepper

broccoli

Brussels sprout

cabbage

carrot

cauliflower

celery

corn

cucumber

eggplant

garlic

ginger

green bean

green onion

kale

42. Vegetables

asparagus

bean

beet

bell pepper

broccoli

Brussels sprout

cabbage

carrot

cauliflower

celery

corn

cucumber

eggplant

garlic

ginger

green bean

green onion

kale

42. Vegetables

lettuce

mushroom

okra

onion

pea

pepper

potato

pumpkin

radish

red onion

spinach

squash

sweet potato

tomato

turnip

yam

zucchini

42. Vegetables

lettuce

mushroom

okra

onion

pea

pepper

potato

pumpkin

radish

red onion

spinach

squash

sweet potato

tomato

turnip

yam

zucchini

43. Food and Drinks

beef

bread

cake

cheese

43. Food and Drinks

beef

bread

cake

cheese

43. Food and Drinks

43. Food and Drinks

chicken	chicken
chips	chips
chocolate	chocolate
coffee	coffee
egg	egg
fries	fries
fruit	fruit
juice	juice
meal	meal
meat	meat
menu	menu
milk	milk
pork	pork
rice	rice
salad	salad
snack	snack
sandwich	sandwich
soda	soda
soup	soup
tea	tea
vegetable	vegetable
water	water

English Grammar

Nouns - Names of People
Singular and Plural Nouns

Nouns - Names of People
Singular and Plural Nouns

baby - babies	baby - babies
boy - boys	boy - boys
child - children	child - children
girl - girls	girl - girls
man - men	man - men
teenager - teenagers	teenager - teenagers
woman - women	woman - women
person - people	person - people
family -families	family -families
friend - friends	friend - friends
neighbor - neighbors	neighbor - neighbors
worker - workers	worker - workers

Nouns - Names of Places

Nouns - Names of Places

airport	airport
apartment	apartment
avenue	avenue
bank	bank
barbershop	barbershop
beach	beach
block	block

Nouns - Names of Places

bookstore	bookstore
bridge	bridge
building	building
bus stop	bus stop
cafe	cafe
cafeteria	cafeteria
canyon	canyon
castle	castle
church	church
city	city
clinic	clinic
convenience store	convenience store
country	country
desert	desert
fire station	fire station
flower shop	flower shop
forest	forest
gas station	gas station
grocery store	grocery store
gym	gym
hill	hill
hospital	hospital
hotel	hotel
house	house

Nouns - Names of Places	Nouns - Names of Places
island	island
lake	lake
library	library
mall	mall
mosque	mosque
mountain	mountain
museum	museum
ocean	ocean
office	office
park	park
pet store	pet store
pharmacy	pharmacy
police station	police station
pool	pool
post office	post office
restroom	restroom
restaurant	restaurant
river	river
road	road
school	school
sea	sea
state	state
street	street
supermarket	supermarket

Nouns - Names of Places

temple	temple
theater	theater
town	town
train station	train station
village	village
zoo	zoo

Nouns - Names of Things

animals	animals
appliances	appliances
clothes	clothes
drinks	drinks
food	food
furniture	furniture
fruits	fruits
money	money
nature	nature
supplies	supplies
technology	technology
toys	toys
utensils	utensils
vegetables	vegetables
vehicles	vehicles

Nouns - Names of Events
Proper and Common Nouns

anniversary

baby shower

birthday

conference

engagement

fundraiser

graduation

housewarming

retirement

reunion

wedding

Christmas

Eid

New Year

Thanksgiving

Valentine's Day

Nouns - Names of Events
Proper and Common Nouns

anniversary

baby shower

birthday

conference

engagement

fundraiser

graduation

housewarming

retirement

reunion

wedding

Christmas

Eid

New Year

Thanksgiving

Valentine's Day

Nouns - Names of Animals

Land Animals

- bear

- cat

- chicken

Nouns - Names of Animals

Land Animals

- bear

- cat

- chicken

Nouns - Names of Animals

Land Animals

- bear
- cat
- chicken
- cow
- deer
- dog
- fox
- frog
- goat
- horse
- lion
- monkey
- mouse
- pig
- rabbit
- sheep
- tiger
- turkey
- wolf

Water Animals

- crab
- dolphin
- fish
- lobster
- octopus

Nouns - Names of Animals

Land Animals

- bear
- cat
- chicken
- cow
- deer
- dog
- fox
- frog
- goat
- horse
- lion
- monkey
- mouse
- pig
- rabbit
- sheep
- tiger
- turkey
- wolf

Water Animals

- crab
- dolphin
- fish
- lobster
- octopus

Nouns - Names of Animals

Water Animals

- seal
- shrimp
- squid
- turtle
- whale

Air Animals

- bee
- bird
- butterfly
- duck
- goose
- owl
- penguin
- pigeon

Nouns - Names of Animals

Water Animals

- seal
- shrimp
- squid
- turtle
- whale

Air Animals

- bee
- bird
- butterfly
- duck
- goose
- owl
- penguin
- pigeon

Pronouns
Subject and Object
Pronouns

I - me

you - you

he - him

she- her

Pronouns
Subject and Object
Pronouns

I - me

you - you

he - him

she- her

Pronouns
Subject and Object
Pronouns

it - it

we - us

they - them

Pronouns
Subject and Object
Pronouns

it - it

we - us

they - them

Verbs

bake

breathe

buy

call

carry

choose

clean

climb

close

cook

count

cross

cry

dance

drink

drive

Verbs

bake

breathe

buy

call

carry

choose

clean

climb

close

cook

count

cross

cry

dance

drink

drive

Verbs	Verbs
dry	dry
eat	eat
exercise	exercise
fasten	fasten
fold	fold
get	get
give	give
go	go
help	help
hug	hug
iron	iron
laugh	laugh
listen	listen
mail	mail
meet	meet
open	open
pass	pass
pay	pay
play	play
pray	pray
pull	pull
push	push
put	put
sleep	sleep

Verbs	Verbs
stop	stop
study	study
read	read
receive	receive
rest	rest
ride	ride
run	run
sew	sew
shop	shop
shower	shower
sing	sing
sit	sit
smile	smile
stand	stand
talk	talk
teach	teach
think	think
turn	turn
walk	walk
wash	wash
wait	wait
wake up	wake up
watch	watch
wear	wear
work	work
write	write

Cooking Action Verbs	Cooking Action Verbs
add	add
bake	bake
blanch	blanch
boil	boil
chop	chop
cook	cook
crack	crack
cut	cut
dice	dice
fry	fry
grate	grate
grill	grill
knead	knead
mash	mash
measure	measure
mince	mince
mix	mix
peel	peel
pour	pour
roast	roast
sauté	sauté
season	season
serve	serve
shred	shred

Cooking Action Verbs

simmer

slice

spread

steam

stew

stir

taste

whisk

Cooking Action Verbs

simmer

slice

spread

steam

stew

stir

taste

whisk

Prepositions

Directions

- in
- inside
- on
- under
- in front of
- at the back of
- behind
- by
- near
- next to
- beside
- close to
- between
- on the right of

Prepositions

Directions

- in
- inside
- on
- under
- in front of
- at the back of
- behind
- by
- near
- next to
- beside
- close to
- between
- on the right of

Prepositions

Directions

- on the left of
- across from
- up
- down
- below
- *above*
- *after*
- *along*
- *at*
- *before*
- *outside*
- *over*
- *from - to*

Directional/Location Words

- *top*
- *bottom*
- *entrance*
- *exit*
- *north*
- *south*
- *east*
- *west*
- *straight ahead*

Prepositions

Directions

- on the left of
- across from
- up
- down
- below
- above
- after
- along
- at
- before
- outside
- over
- from - to

Directional/Location Words

- top
- bottom
- entrance
- exit
- north
- south
- east
- west
- straight ahead

Adjectives

big

busy

calm

cold

fast

happy

hot

long

loud

new

old

quiet

sad

short

small

slow

soft

tall

tasty

Size

- *extra small*
- *small*
- *medium*
- *large*
- *extra large*

Adjectives

big

busy

calm

cold

fast

happy

hot

long

loud

new

old

quiet

sad

short

small

slow

soft

tall

tasty

Size

- extra small
- small
- medium
- large
- extra large

Adjectives

House Problems

- *broken*
- *clogged*
- *dirty*
- *leaky*
- *noisy*
- *rusty*
- *smelly*
- *stuck*
- *wet*
- *worn out*

Adjectives

House Problems

- broken
- clogged
- dirty
- leaky
- noisy
- rusty
- smelly
- stuck
- wet
- worn out

Opposites

up - down
hot - cold
close - open
happy - sad
on - off
old - new
full - empty
day - night
big - small
tall - short
soft - hard

Opposites

up - down
hot - cold
close - open
happy - sad
on - off
old – new
full - empty
day – night
big - small
tall - short
soft – hard

Opposites

long - short
out - in
slow - fast
young - old
stop - go
sunny - rainy

Opposites

long - short
out - in
slow - fast
young - old
stop - go
sunny - rainy

Conjunctions

and
because
but
if
or
so
when
while
yet

Conjunctions

and
because
but
if
or
so
when
while
yet

Adverbs of Frequency (How often?)

always — 100%
daily — 100%
usually — 80-90%
generally — 70-80%

Adverbs of Frequency
(How often?)

always — 100%
daily — 100%
usually — 80-90%
generally — 70-80%

**Adverbs of Frequency
(How often?)**

often — 50-70%

sometimes — 30-50%

occasionally — 10-30%

once a week — about 14%

twice a month — about 7%

rarely — 5-10%

seldom — 1-5%

never — 0%

Adverbs of Time (When?)

early

every day

now

on weekends

Adverbs of Frequency
(How often?)

often — 50-70%

sometimes — 30-50%

occasionally — 10-30%

once a week — about 14%

twice a month — about 7%

rarely — 5-10%

seldom — 1-5%

never — 0%

Adverbs of Time (When?)

early

every day

now

on weekends

Adverbs of Time (When?)

soon

this morning

today

tomorrow

tonight

yesterday

Adverbs of Time (When?)

soon

this morning

today

tomorrow

tonight

yesterday

Adverbs of Manner (How?)

carefully

fast

hard

quietly

quickly

slowly

well

Adverbs of Manner (How?)

carefully

fast

hard

quietly

quickly

slowly

well

Symbols and Punctuation Marks

& ampersand (and)

' apostrophe

, comma

$ dollar sign

. dot

. period

= equals

! exclamation point

hashtag

pound

number

- hyphen

- minus

( ) parentheses

Symbols and Punctuation Marks

& ampersand (and)

' apostrophe

, comma

$ dollar sign

. dot

. period

= equals

! exclamation point

hashtag

pound

number

- hyphen

- minus

( ) parentheses

Symbols and Punctuation Marks

+ plus

" " quotation marks

/ slash

@ at

? question mark

Symbols and Punctuation Marks

+ plus

" " quotation marks

/ slash

@ at

? question mark

NOTES

CEFR Levels and U.S. ESL Equivalents
Vocabulary Descriptions from A1 to C2

CEFR Level	U.S. ESL Equivalent	Vocabulary Description
A1	ESL Literacy / ESL Level 1	Can recognize and use very basic everyday words and expressions.
A2	ESL Level 2	Can use common words related to everyday life, such as food, family, and jobs.
B1	ESL Levels 3–4 (Low-Intermediate)	Can use vocabulary for school, work, travel, and simple opinions.
B2	ESL Levels 5–6 (High Intermediate)	Can use a wide range of general, academic, and workplace vocabulary with growing confidence.
C1	College ESL / University Prep	Can use precise, academic, and professional vocabulary confidently.
C2	Near-native / Advanced Fluency	Can understand and use nearly all vocabulary in any context.